21st Century Junior Library

Allosaurus

by Lucia Raatma

CHERRY LAKE PUBLISHING * ANN ARBOR, MICHIGAN

Published in the United States of America by Cherry Lake Publishing
Ann Arbor, Michigan
www.cherrylakepublishing.com

Content Adviser: Gregory M. Erickson, PhD, Dinosaur Paleontologist, Department of Biological
Science, Florida State University, Tallahassee, Florida

Reading Adviser: Marla Conn, Read with Me Now

Photo Credits: Cover and pages 4 and 18, ©Image Source/Alamy; page 6, ©STT0007390/Media
Bakery; page 8, ©Eye Risk/Alamy; page 10 top, ©Universal Images Group Limited/Alamy; page 10
bottom, ©Rob Wilson/Shutterstock, Inc.; page 12, ©Jean-Michel Girard/Shutterstock, Inc.; page 14,
©STT0006463/Media Bakery; page 16, ©STT0006230/Media Bakery; page 20, ©Travelscape
Images/Alamy

LIBRARY OF CONGRESS CATALOGING-IN-PUBLICATION DATA

Raatma, Lucia.
 Allosaurus/by Lucia Raatma.
   p. cm.—(21st century junior library) (Dinosaurs)
 Includes bibliographical references and index.
 ISBN 978-1-61080-466-0 (lib. bdg.)—ISBN 978-1-61080-553-7 (e-book)—
ISBN 978-1-61080-640-4 (pbk.)
 1. Allosaurus—Juvenile literature. I. Title.
 QE862.S3R327 2013
 567.912—dc23   2012004212

*Cherry Lake Publishing would like to acknowledge the work of
The Partnership for 21st Century Skills.
Please visit* www.21stcenturyskills.org *for more information.*

Printed in the United States of America
Corporate Graphics Inc.
July 2012
CLFA11

CONTENTS

A hungry *Allosaurus* was a dangerous animal.

What Was an Allosaurus?

Imagine being a young dinosaur living in an ancient forest. A big, meat-eating dinosaur is chasing you! It might be an *Allosaurus*. This powerful **predator** lived about 150 million years ago. Like other dinosaurs, the *Allosaurus* is now **extinct**.

Allosaurus lived in what is now
the United States.

Where did the name *Allosaurus* come from? It is a word that means "different lizard." Why did scientists choose that name? It's because the *Allosaurus* had features like no other dinosaur. The *Allosaurus* lived in western North America. It may also have lived in Europe and Africa.

Think!

When you think about dinosaurs, what do you picture? Do you see a gentle animal eating plants? Or do you imagine a scary creature with big, sharp teeth?

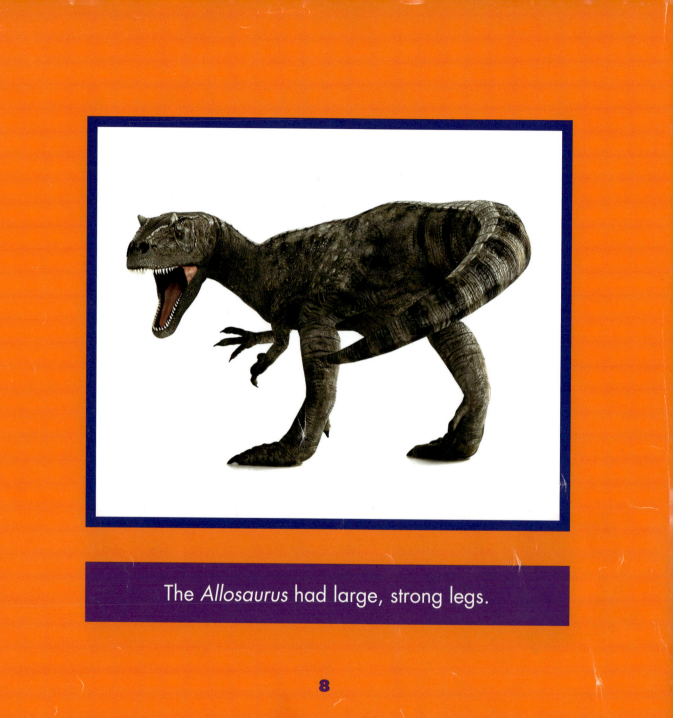

The *Allosaurus* had large, strong legs.

What Did an Allosaurus Look Like?

The *Allosaurus* had powerful legs and short arms. Each hand had three fingers. Each finger had a claw. A claw could be as long as 11 inches (28 centimeters). This dinosaur had a bulky body and a big tail.

An *Allosaurus* was about as long as a school bus.

This fierce dinosaur was about 38 feet (11.6 meters) long and as tall as 16.5 feet (5 m). Most *Allosaurus* weighed between 1 and 3 tons. That is about as heavy as a car.

The *Allosaurus* was a fierce fighter with its sharp teeth and claws.

The *Allosaurus* had heavy bones. Its thick neck was shaped like an S. Its skull was about 3 feet (1 m) long. There were bony ridges above each eye. Its jaws were strong. It had sharp teeth that were 2 to 4 inches (5 to 10 cm) long.

Look!

Pay attention next time you are in a hardware store. Look at the nails. The *Allosaurus* had teeth as long and sharp as some nails!

An *Allosaurus* could hunt dinosaurs that were larger than it was.

How Did an Allosaurus Live?

The *Allosaurus* was a dangerous **carnivore**. It hunted and ate other dinosaurs. It used its powerful jaws and sharp teeth. The huge *Stegosaurus* and *Apatosaurus* were some of its **prey**. The *Allosaurus* may also have targeted young dinosaurs that were weaker.

These two *Allosaurus* have hunted
down a *Stegosaurus*.

You may wonder how the *Allosaurus* could hunt larger dinosaurs. This predator likely hunted in **herds**. A group of *Allosaurus* could corner a large *Stegosaurus* and attack it. Even a big dinosaur could not defend itself against an *Allosaurus* herd.

Ask Questions!

Talk to your friends and family. Do they feel stronger and safer in a group? Do any of them prefer not to go out alone? Imagine why the *Allosaurus* hunted in groups.

Allosaurus usually did not move very fast.

The *Allosaurus* was not a fast runner. Its **stride** was about 9 feet (3 m) long. Scientists believe that it moved slowly on its two huge legs. This was because an *Allosaurus* might fall while running. Its short arms would not be able to stop the fall. Then the dinosaur would hurt its head.

Scientists who study fossils are
called paleontologists.

All *Allosaurus* are extinct. How do we know about the *Allosaurus*? Scientists study **fossils**. Many of these fossils were discovered in Colorado and Utah in the United States. Scientists are still learning about this large, dangerous animal. What will they find out next? Will you be the one to discover it?

Create!

Ask an adult for a box of toothpicks and some glue. Try making a small dinosaur skeleton with these materials. Now think about scientists assembling dinosaur fossils. How hard do you think it is to do this?

GLOSSARY

carnivore (KAHR-nuh-vor) an animal that eats meat

extinct (ek-STINGKT) describing a type of plant or animal that has completely died out

fossils (FAH-suhlz) the preserved remains of living things from thousands or millions of years ago

herds (HURDZ) large groups of animals

predator (PRED-uh-tur) an animal that lives by hunting other animals for food

prey (PRAY) an animal that is hunted by other animals for food

stride (STRIDE) the length between an animal's feet when it walks or runs

FIND OUT MORE

BOOKS

Gray, Susan Heinrichs. *Allosaurus.* Mankato, MN: The Child's World, 2010.

Rockwood, Leigh. *Allosaurus.* New York: PowerKids Press, 2012.

WEB SITES

Denver Museum of Nature & Science: Prehistoric Journey
www.dmns.org/exhibitions/ current-exhibitions/prehistoric-journey Travel through time and watch *Allosaurus* and *Stegosaurus* in battle.

San Diego Natural History Museum: Fossil Mysteries
www.sdnhm.org/exhibitions/ current-exhibitions/fossil-mysteries/ Learn about the dinosaur fossils on display.

INDEX

ABOUT THE AUTHOR

Lucia Raatma has written dozens of books for young readers. She and her family live in the Tampa Bay area of Florida. They enjoy looking at the dinosaur fossils at the local science museum.